KB093753

Stay Series 1

STAY IN DAEDONG

대
동
에

머
물
다

2019년 봄부터 대전 동구에 있는 작은 동네 대동에 머물렀다. 머무는 동안 자주 걸었다. 꽤 여러 번 셔터를 누르면서 발길이 이끄는 대로 흘러가는 시간을 잡아두었다. 놓칠까 봐 두려운 시간도, 마주하기 버거운 시간도 있었다. 그저 마음에 닿은 순간을 외면하지 않으려 애썼다.

대동에서 다섯 번째 봄을 보내고 나서야 이 책을 엮을 수 있었다. 사라지는 시간을 붙잡는 데는 대개 1/250초면 충분했다. 이 책에 담긴 사진은 대부분 필름으로 찍었다. 필름 값이 갈수록 올라 점점 더디게 걷는 요즘이지만, 여전히 나는 대동에 머물고 있다. 이곳에 오래도록 머무는 내 마음이 부디 당신에게도 잘 전달되었으면.

———

Since spring 2019, I have dwelled in a small village called Daedong, in Donggu (East District) Daejeon. Dwelling in this village, I often take walks. Pressing the shutter button of my camera, I captured moments as my feet took me around Daedong. During those times, there were moments that I was afraid of missing and moments that were hard to absorb. I tried to not turn away those moments that touched my heart.

I made this book after spending 5 spring seasons in Daedong. 1/250 of a second was enough to capture those disappearing moments. Most of the photographs in this book were taken with film cameras. I am still staying in Daedong, but I take less photographs because the price of film has increased. I hope my feelings of staying in Daedong go out to you.

대동을 거닐 때면 뜻밖의 풍경을 종종 만난다. 고추장 통이나 고무 대야, 부서진 욕조, 심지어 변기에 심긴 꽃이나 어느 틈에 자란 심지도 않은 풀들. 예상치 못한 곳에서 만나 피식 웃게 하는 고양이들. 따사로운 햇볕과 그늘의 적절한 경계에 놓인 의자들. 집 앞의 주차를 막는 저마다의 기발한 장애물들. 그중에 무엇보다 좋은 풍경은 때때마다 피어나는 색색의 꽃잎들.

대동과 사랑에 빠지는 데는 그리 오랜 시간이 걸리지 않는다.

———

Wandering about Daedong, I often encounter unexpected scenes such as flowers planted in the jar of Gochujang, flowers in a big washbasin, or even flowers planted in the toilet. Grass is growing through a crack in concrete, and stray cats that come out from nowhere make me smile. Some chairs on the horizon between the cool shade and the warm sunlight. Brilliant obstacles in front of each house that claim their parking spot. The most amazing scenes are various colors of flowers in different seasons.

It doesn't take a long time to fall in love with Daedong.

아름다운 순간을 붙잡고자 애쓰던 시간을 지나, 무너지는 풍경을 자주 마주했다. 돌이킬 수도, 돌아갈 수도 없는 시간들이 자꾸만 쌓였다. 조급한 마음이 들었다. 시간의 흐름과 자연의 섭리로 받아들이기에는 힘든 나날도 많았다. 그저 내가 할 수 있는 일을 했다. 마음이 지나는 곳을 따라 몇 장의 사진만 남았다.

———

Over this time, I've tried hard to capture the beautiful moments, but I faced disappearing moments. Those moments have accumulated. I can't go back and I can't reflect. I feel rushed. Those moments were hard to accept as a way of nature, or the passage of time. I just did what I could do. I left photographs of moments where my heart lingered.

파란 하늘 위에 뭉게구름이 피어오를 때나 하늘공원 가득히 꽃이 만개
했을 때, 기막힌 빛깔의 노을이 지붕들 위로 펼쳐졌을 때처럼 행운이 도
래한 순간을 자주 목격했다. 숨이 차고 땀에 젖을 때까지 오르막길을 달
려도 마냥 좋은 순간. 가끔은 벅차오르는 풍경 앞에서 소리 내는 법을
잊기도 했다.

———

I was lucky to witness the moments when the blue sky was
filled with fluffy clouds, when the sky park was full of flowers,
and when there were stunning colors of sunsets over the roofs
of houses. When those moments come, I run up the hill of this
village until I am out of breath and soaked in sweat. Encountering
these overwhelming scenes, I was speechless.

대동에서 몇 번의 계절 속에 머무는 동안 두고두고 잊지 못할 시간을 걸었다. 이 걸음이 오래도록 이어지기를, 소박하고도 풍요로운 장면을 계속 발견할 수 있기를, 간절히 바랄 뿐이다.

———

While I am staying in the seasons of Daedong, I walked through some unforgettable moments. I hope very much I can keep wandering about here and keep discovering rustic, but abundant moments.

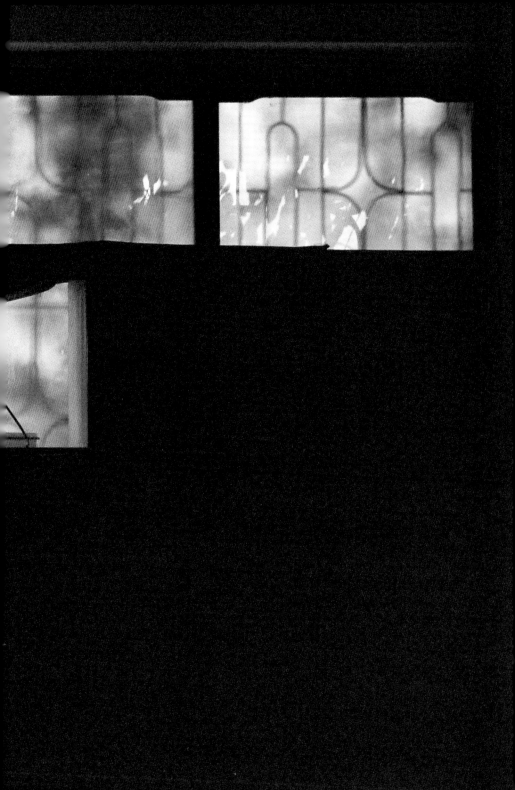

Stay Series

머물다가게의 출판사 다니그라피에서
만드는 머물다 시리즈입니다.
어딘가에 혹은 무언가에 오래도록 머물며
기록한 이야기를 담습니다.

———

임다은
조금 낡고 느린 것을 좋아합니다.
먼 훗날의 유물을 만듭니다.
@dani_graphy

Stay Series

Meomulda(Stay) Series is published by
Meomulda Shop's publisher, Dani-graphy.
Meomulda series is a story about staying for
a long time in somewhere or something.

———

Lim Da Eun
I like something old and slow.
I make artifacts for the distant future.
@dani_graphy

STAY IN DAEDONG
대동에 머물다

초판 1쇄 발행 2023년 10월 13일

사진·글 임다은
영문번역 이솔, 콜
편집디자인 임다은
펴낸이 임다은
펴낸곳 다니그라피
출판등록 제2019-000012호 (2019.5.31)
주소 대전시 동구 대동로 44, 1층 머물다가게
전화 070-8098-6634
이메일 meomuldashop@naver.com
블로그 blog.naver.com/meomuldashop
인스타그램 @meomuldashop / @dngrp

ISBN 979-11-970721-8-5
값 25,000원

ⓒ 임다은, 2023

Published in October 13, 2023

Photo·Wirte Lim Da Eun
Translation by Lee Sol, Cole Bearden
Edited by Lim Da Eun
Publisher Lim Da Eun
Published by Dani-graphy
Publication registration No. 2019-000012
Address 44 Daedong-ro, Dong-gu, Daejeon
Phone 070-8098-6634
E-mail meomuldashop@naver.com
Blog blog.naver.com/meomuldashop
Instagram @meomuldashop / @dngrp

ISBN 979-11-970721-8-5
Price 25,000won

ⓒ Lim Da Eun, 2023